FACT ATTACK

AWESOME ALIENS

Ian Locke

MACMILLAN CHILDREN'S BOOKS

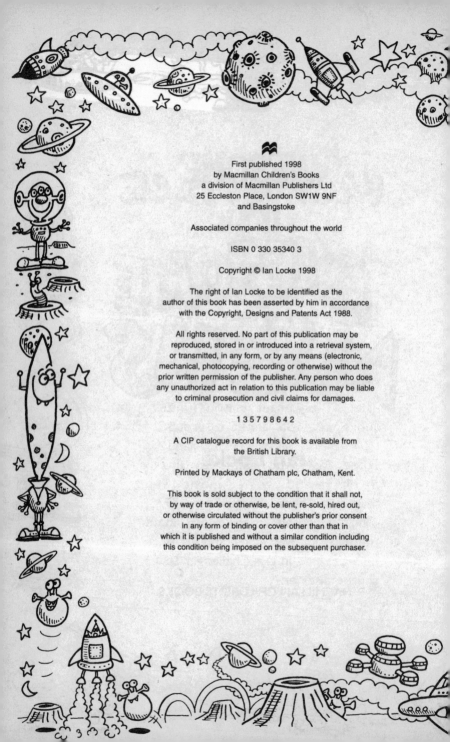

First published 1998
by Macmillan Children's Books
a division of Macmillan Publishers Ltd
25 Eccleston Place, London SW1W 9NF
and Basingstoke

Associated companies throughout the world

ISBN 0 330 35340 3

1 3 5 7 9 8 6 4 2

A CIP catalogue record for this book is available from
the British Library.

Printed by Mackays of Chatham plc, Chatham, Kent.

AWESOME ALIENS

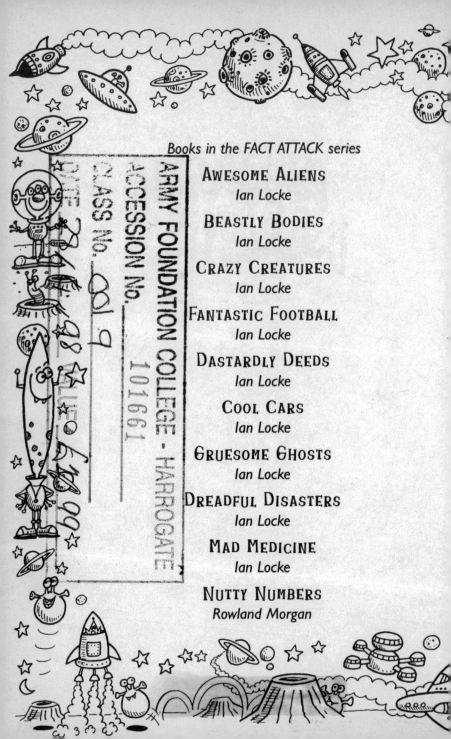

Books in the FACT ATTACK series

AWESOME ALIENS
Ian Locke

BEASTLY BODIES
Ian Locke

CRAZY CREATURES
Ian Locke

FANTASTIC FOOTBALL
Ian Locke

DASTARDLY DEEDS
Ian Locke

COOL CARS
Ian Locke

GRUESOME GHOSTS
Ian Locke

DREADFUL DISASTERS
Ian Locke

MAD MEDICINE
Ian Locke

NUTTY NUMBERS
Rowland Morgan

AWESOME ALIENS

DID YOU KNOW THAT . . .

★ The US astronaut Ellison Onizuka spoke in 1985 about a group of US Air Force pilots at McClelland Air Force Base who had been shown a black and white movie film featuring "alien bodies" in 1973. Onizuka agreed to say more about the film, but was never able to since he was killed in the Challenger space shuttle disaster.

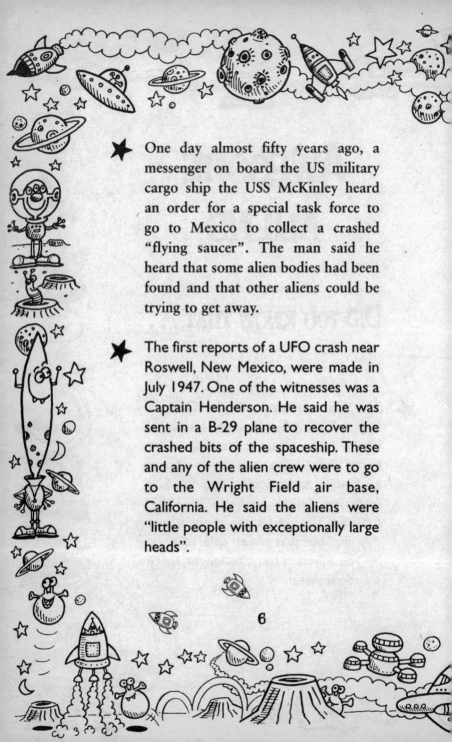

★ One day almost fifty years ago, a messenger on board the US military cargo ship the USS McKinley heard an order for a special task force to go to Mexico to collect a crashed "flying saucer". The man said he heard that some alien bodies had been found and that other aliens could be trying to get away.

★ The first reports of a UFO crash near Roswell, New Mexico, were made in July 1947. One of the witnesses was a Captain Henderson. He said he was sent in a B-29 plane to recover the crashed bits of the spaceship. These and any of the alien crew were to go to the Wright Field air base, California. He said the aliens were "little people with exceptionally large heads".

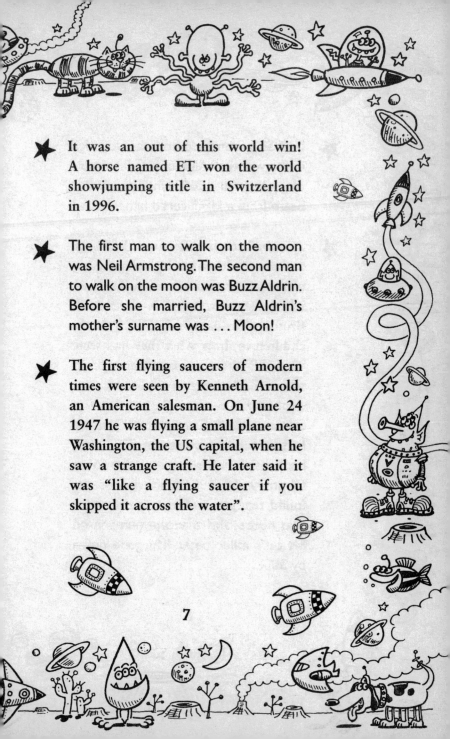

★ It was an out of this world win! A horse named ET won the world showjumping title in Switzerland in 1996.

★ The first man to walk on the moon was Neil Armstrong. The second man to walk on the moon was Buzz Aldrin. Before she married, Buzz Aldrin's mother's surname was ... Moon!

★ The first flying saucers of modern times were seen by Kenneth Arnold, an American salesman. On June 24 1947 he was flying a small plane near Washington, the US capital, when he saw a strange craft. He later said it was "like a flying saucer if you skipped it across the water".

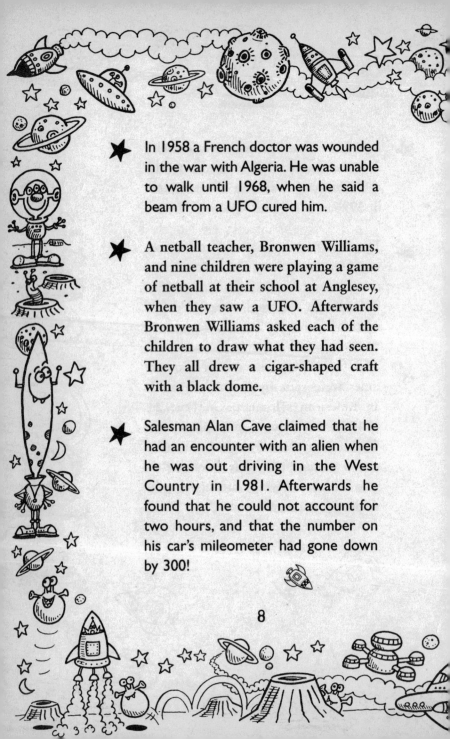

★ In 1958 a French doctor was wounded in the war with Algeria. He was unable to walk until 1968, when he said a beam from a UFO cured him.

★ A netball teacher, Bronwen Williams, and nine children were playing a game of netball at their school at Anglesey, when they saw a UFO. Afterwards Bronwen Williams asked each of the children to draw what they had seen. They all drew a cigar-shaped craft with a black dome.

★ Salesman Alan Cave claimed that he had an encounter with an alien when he was out driving in the West Country in 1981. Afterwards he found that he could not account for two hours, and that the number on his car's mileometer had gone down by 300!

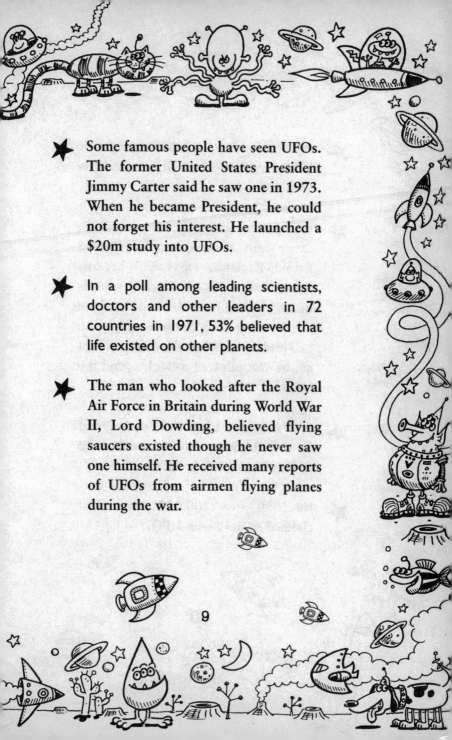

★ Some famous people have seen UFOs. The former United States President Jimmy Carter said he saw one in 1973. When he became President, he could not forget his interest. He launched a $20m study into UFOs.

★ In a poll among leading scientists, doctors and other leaders in 72 countries in 1971, 53% believed that life existed on other planets.

★ The man who looked after the Royal Air Force in Britain during World War II, Lord Dowding, believed flying saucers existed though he never saw one himself. He received many reports of UFOs from airmen flying planes during the war.

9

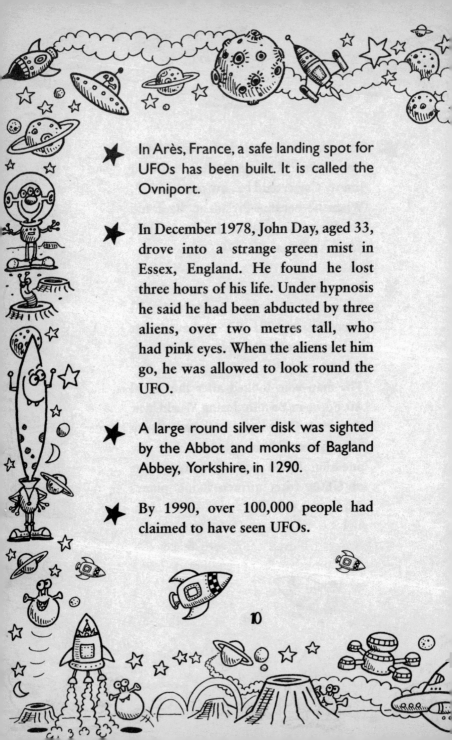

★ In Arès, France, a safe landing spot for UFOs has been built. It is called the Ovniport.

★ In December 1978, John Day, aged 33, drove into a strange green mist in Essex, England. He found he lost three hours of his life. Under hypnosis he said he had been abducted by three aliens, over two metres tall, who had pink eyes. When the aliens let him go, he was allowed to look round the UFO.

★ A large round silver disk was sighted by the Abbot and monks of Bagland Abbey, Yorkshire, in 1290.

★ By 1990, over 100,000 people had claimed to have seen UFOs.

★ A family from Gloucester seem to have been abducted by aliens in June 1978. As they drove towards the top of a hill, they saw a white light in the sky. They heard a noise, and a huge saucer-like object approached. They could not remember anything else. They just drove home. There they phoned the police and told them about the UFO. They realized there was an hour missing from their journey. Over the next few days the family were affected by itchy skin and strange bruises. The parents went to a hypnotist. When in a deep sleep, they said the family had been abducted by aliens from a planet called Janos. The aliens said they could share their secrets in return for a place to live on Earth. Doctors and scientists checked the story. They decided the parents believed they were telling the truth about what happened during that missing hour.

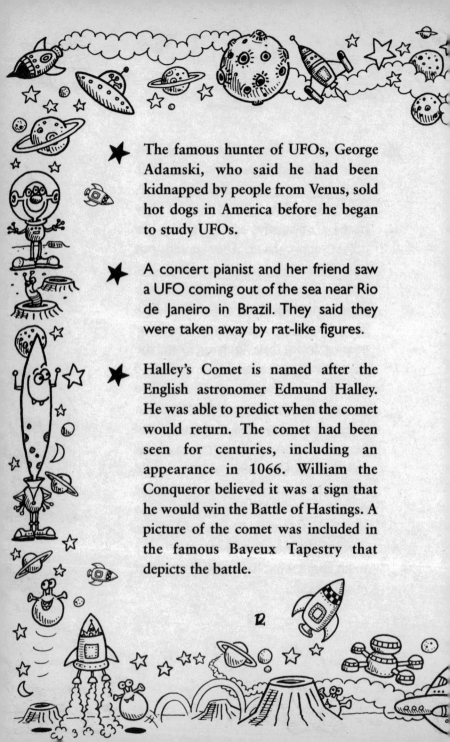

The famous hunter of UFOs, George Adamski, who said he had been kidnapped by people from Venus, sold hot dogs in America before he began to study UFOs.

A concert pianist and her friend saw a UFO coming out of the sea near Rio de Janeiro in Brazil. They said they were taken away by rat-like figures.

Halley's Comet is named after the English astronomer Edmund Halley. He was able to predict when the comet would return. The comet had been seen for centuries, including an appearance in 1066. William the Conqueror believed it was a sign that he would win the Battle of Hastings. A picture of the comet was included in the famous Bayeux Tapestry that depicts the battle.

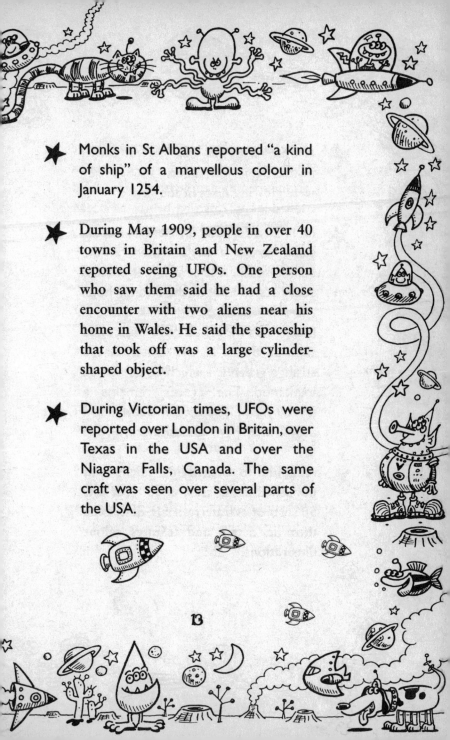

★ Monks in St Albans reported "a kind of ship" of a marvellous colour in January 1254.

★ During May 1909, people in over 40 towns in Britain and New Zealand reported seeing UFOs. One person who saw them said he had a close encounter with two aliens near his home in Wales. He said the spaceship that took off was a large cylinder-shaped object.

★ During Victorian times, UFOs were reported over London in Britain, over Texas in the USA and over the Niagara Falls, Canada. The same craft was seen over several parts of the USA.

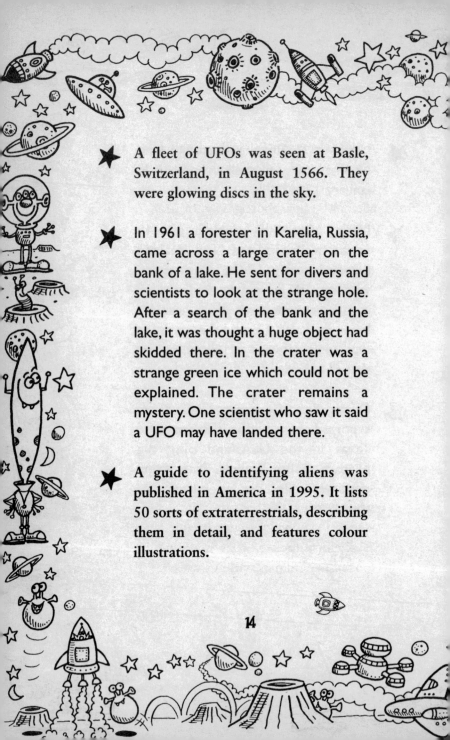

★ A fleet of UFOs was seen at Basle, Switzerland, in August 1566. They were glowing discs in the sky.

★ In 1961 a forester in Karelia, Russia, came across a large crater on the bank of a lake. He sent for divers and scientists to look at the strange hole. After a search of the bank and the lake, it was thought a huge object had skidded there. In the crater was a strange green ice which could not be explained. The crater remains a mystery. One scientist who saw it said a UFO may have landed there.

★ A guide to identifying aliens was published in America in 1995. It lists 50 sorts of extraterrestrials, describing them in detail, and features colour illustrations.

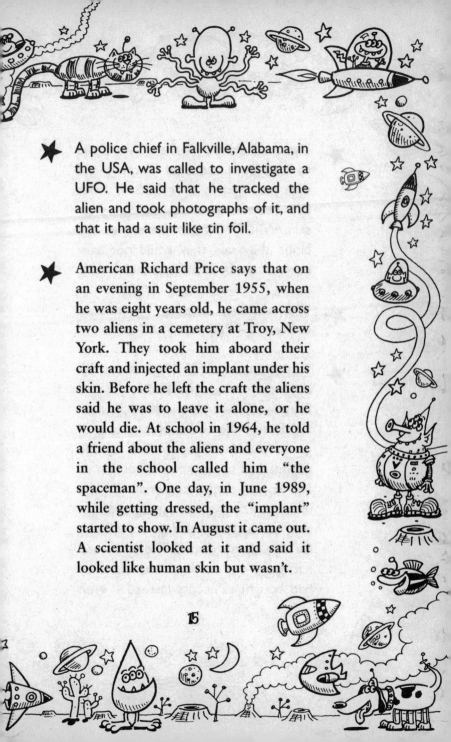

★ A police chief in Falkville, Alabama, in the USA, was called to investigate a UFO. He said that he tracked the alien and took photographs of it, and that it had a suit like tin foil.

★ American Richard Price says that on an evening in September 1955, when he was eight years old, he came across two aliens in a cemetery at Troy, New York. They took him aboard their craft and injected an implant under his skin. Before he left the craft the aliens said he was to leave it alone, or he would die. At school in 1964, he told a friend about the aliens and everyone in the school called him "the spaceman". One day, in June 1989, while getting dressed, the "implant" started to show. In August it came out. A scientist looked at it and said it looked like human skin but wasn't.

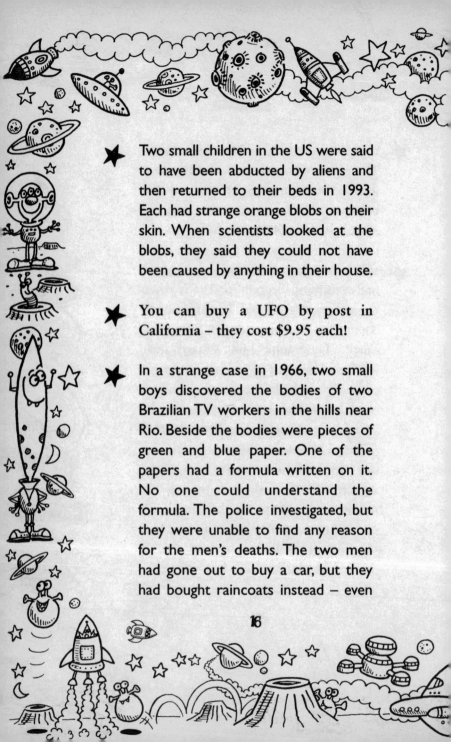

★ Two small children in the US were said to have been abducted by aliens and then returned to their beds in 1993. Each had strange orange blobs on their skin. When scientists looked at the blobs, they said they could not have been caused by anything in their house.

★ You can buy a UFO by post in California – they cost $9.95 each!

★ In a strange case in 1966, two small boys discovered the bodies of two Brazilian TV workers in the hills near Rio. Beside the bodies were pieces of green and blue paper. One of the papers had a formula written on it. No one could understand the formula. The police investigated, but they were unable to find any reason for the men's deaths. The two men had gone out to buy a car, but they had bought raincoats instead – even

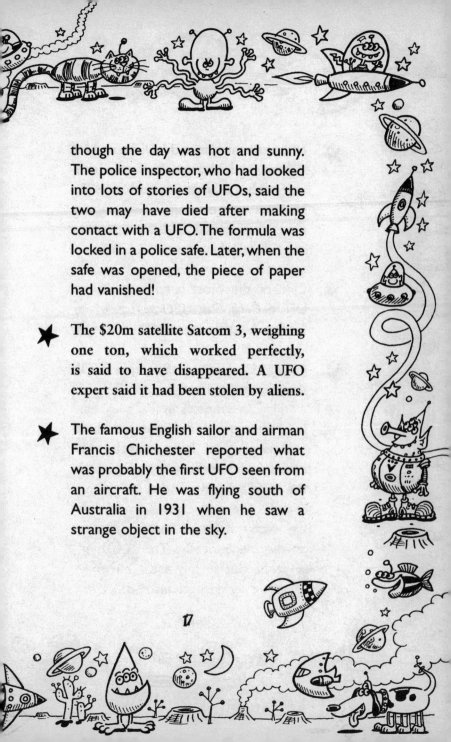

though the day was hot and sunny. The police inspector, who had looked into lots of stories of UFOs, said the two may have died after making contact with a UFO. The formula was locked in a police safe. Later, when the safe was opened, the piece of paper had vanished!

★ The $20m satellite Satcom 3, weighing one ton, which worked perfectly, is said to have disappeared. A UFO expert said it had been stolen by aliens.

★ The famous English sailor and airman Francis Chichester reported what was probably the first UFO seen from an aircraft. He was flying south of Australia in 1931 when he saw a strange object in the sky.

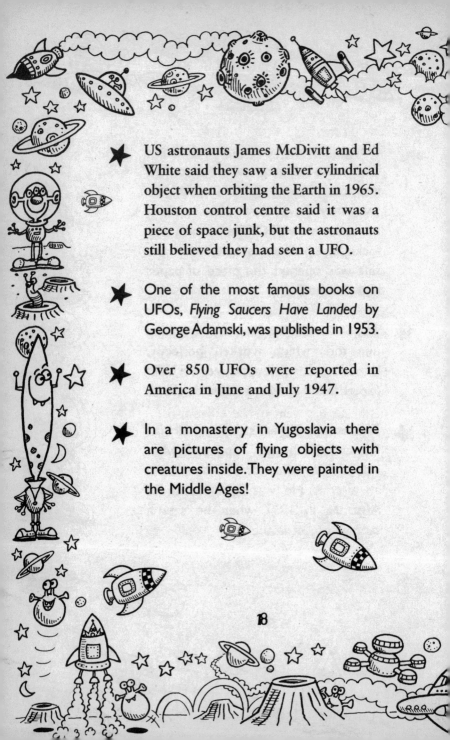

★ US astronauts James McDivitt and Ed White said they saw a silver cylindrical object when orbiting the Earth in 1965. Houston control centre said it was a piece of space junk, but the astronauts still believed they had seen a UFO.

★ One of the most famous books on UFOs, *Flying Saucers Have Landed* by George Adamski, was published in 1953.

★ Over 850 UFOs were reported in America in June and July 1947.

★ In a monastery in Yugoslavia there are pictures of flying objects with creatures inside. They were painted in the Middle Ages!

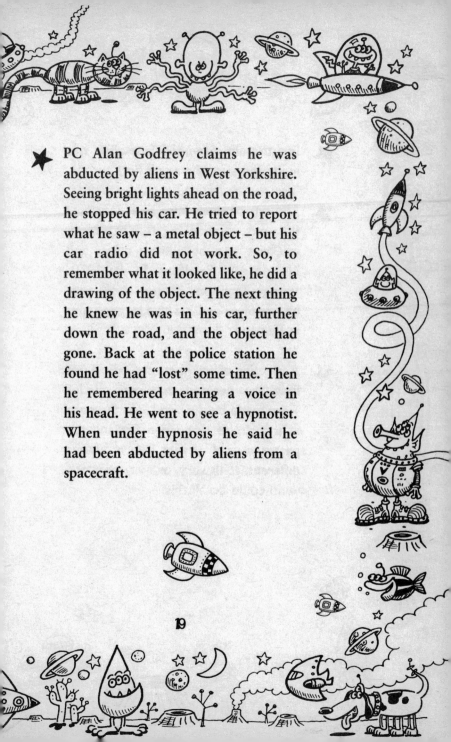

PC Alan Godfrey claims he was abducted by aliens in West Yorkshire. Seeing bright lights ahead on the road, he stopped his car. He tried to report what he saw – a metal object – but his car radio did not work. So, to remember what it looked like, he did a drawing of the object. The next thing he knew he was in his car, further down the road, and the object had gone. Back at the police station he found he had "lost" some time. Then he remembered hearing a voice in his head. He went to see a hypnotist. When under hypnosis he said he had been abducted by aliens from a spacecraft.

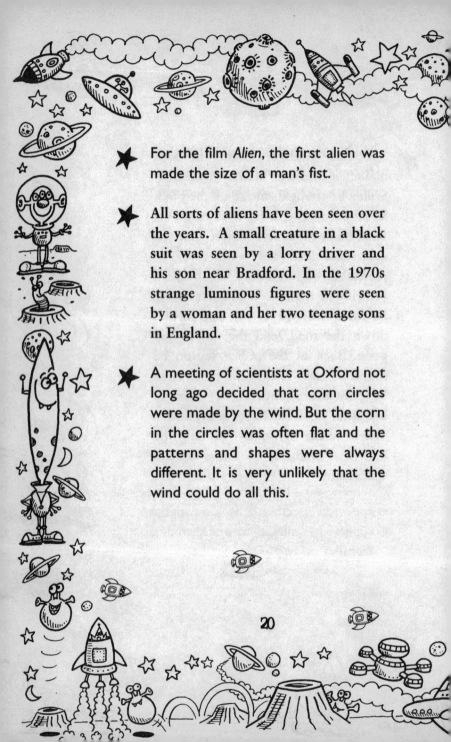

★ For the film *Alien*, the first alien was made the size of a man's fist.

★ All sorts of aliens have been seen over the years. A small creature in a black suit was seen by a lorry driver and his son near Bradford. In the 1970s strange luminous figures were seen by a woman and her two teenage sons in England.

★ A meeting of scientists at Oxford not long ago decided that corn circles were made by the wind. But the corn in the circles was often flat and the patterns and shapes were always different. It is very unlikely that the wind could do all this.

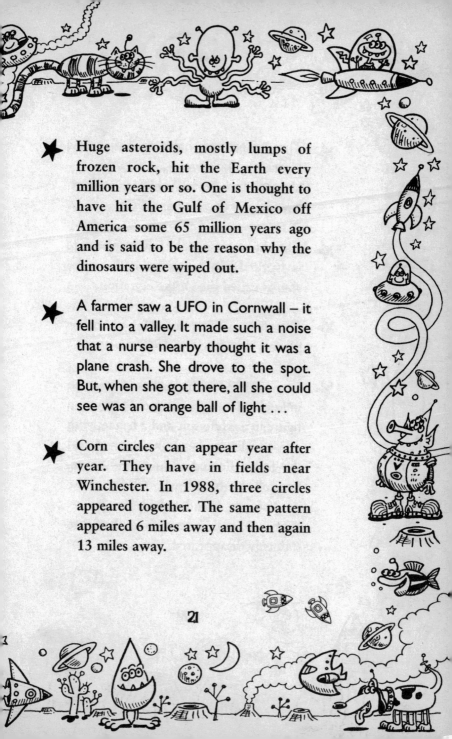

Huge asteroids, mostly lumps of frozen rock, hit the Earth every million years or so. One is thought to have hit the Gulf of Mexico off America some 65 million years ago and is said to be the reason why the dinosaurs were wiped out.

A farmer saw a UFO in Cornwall – it fell into a valley. It made such a noise that a nurse nearby thought it was a plane crash. She drove to the spot. But, when she got there, all she could see was an orange ball of light ...

Corn circles can appear year after year. They have in fields near Winchester. In 1988, three circles appeared together. The same pattern appeared 6 miles away and then again 13 miles away.

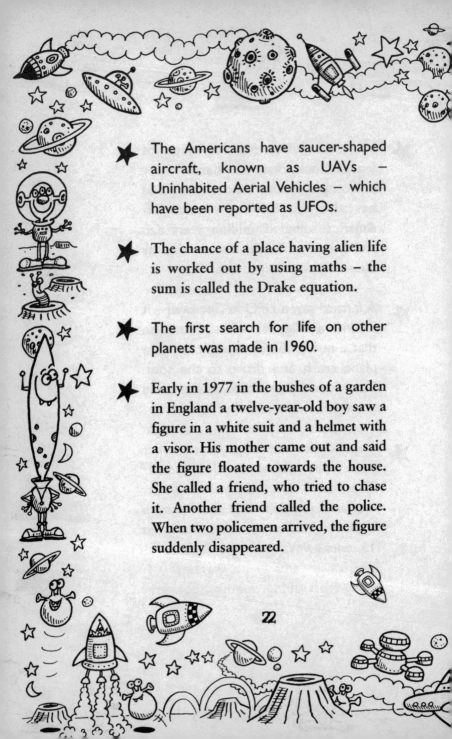

★ The Americans have saucer-shaped aircraft, known as UAVs – Uninhabited Aerial Vehicles – which have been reported as UFOs.

★ The chance of a place having alien life is worked out by using maths – the sum is called the Drake equation.

★ The first search for life on other planets was made in 1960.

★ Early in 1977 in the bushes of a garden in England a twelve-year-old boy saw a figure in a white suit and a helmet with a visor. His mother came out and said the figure floated towards the house. She called a friend, who tried to chase it. Another friend called the police. When two policemen arrived, the figure suddenly disappeared.

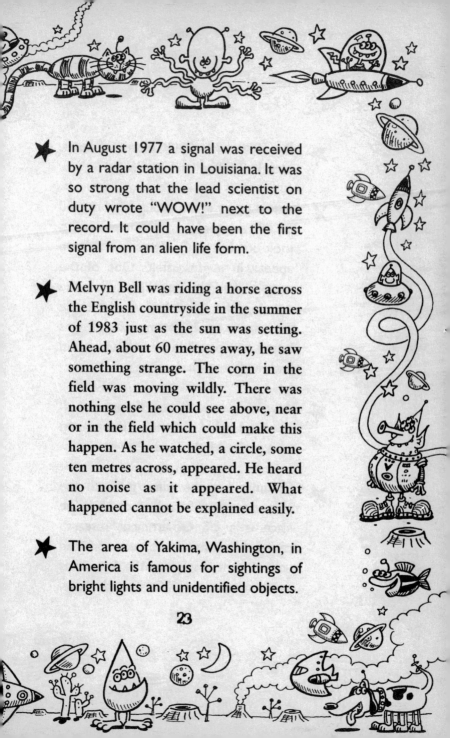

★ In August 1977 a signal was received by a radar station in Louisiana. It was so strong that the lead scientist on duty wrote "WOW!" next to the record. It could have been the first signal from an alien life form.

★ Melvyn Bell was riding a horse across the English countryside in the summer of 1983 just as the sun was setting. Ahead, about 60 metres away, he saw something strange. The corn in the field was moving wildly. There was nothing else he could see above, near or in the field which could make this happen. As he watched, a circle, some ten metres across, appeared. He heard no noise as it appeared. What happened cannot be explained easily.

★ The area of Yakima, Washington, in America is famous for sightings of bright lights and unidentified objects.

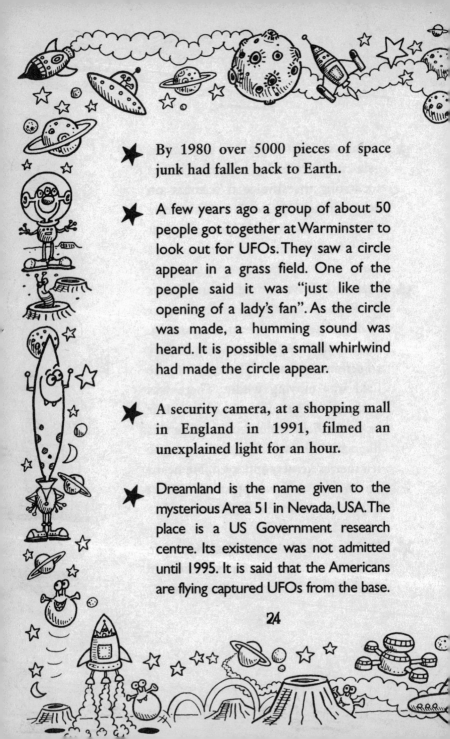

★ By 1980 over 5000 pieces of space junk had fallen back to Earth.

★ A few years ago a group of about 50 people got together at Warminster to look out for UFOs. They saw a circle appear in a grass field. One of the people said it was "just like the opening of a lady's fan". As the circle was made, a humming sound was heard. It is possible a small whirlwind had made the circle appear.

★ A security camera, at a shopping mall in England in 1991, filmed an unexplained light for an hour.

★ Dreamland is the name given to the mysterious Area 51 in Nevada, USA. The place is a US Government research centre. Its existence was not admitted until 1995. It is said that the Americans are flying captured UFOs from the base.

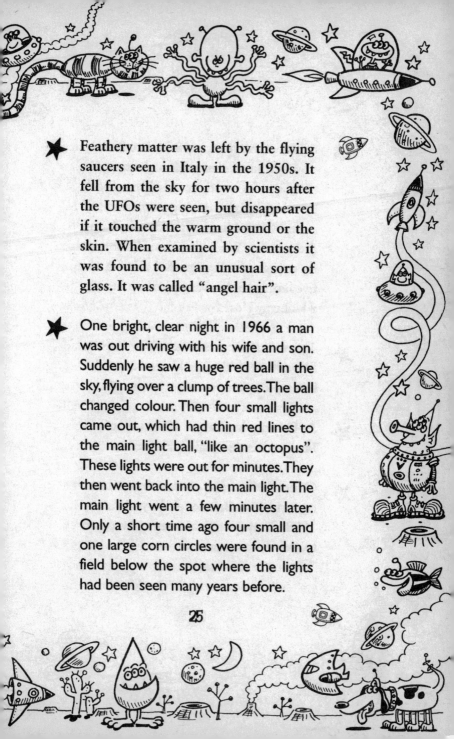

Feathery matter was left by the flying saucers seen in Italy in the 1950s. It fell from the sky for two hours after the UFOs were seen, but disappeared if it touched the warm ground or the skin. When examined by scientists it was found to be an unusual sort of glass. It was called "angel hair".

One bright, clear night in 1966 a man was out driving with his wife and son. Suddenly he saw a huge red ball in the sky, flying over a clump of trees. The ball changed colour. Then four small lights came out, which had thin red lines to the main light ball, "like an octopus". These lights were out for minutes. They then went back into the main light. The main light went a few minutes later. Only a short time ago four small and one large corn circles were found in a field below the spot where the lights had been seen many years before.

An American man, out with two friends, says he had an encounter with aliens. At the edge of a wood, he was thrown back by a bright light. A little later an object stunned him. His two friends ran off and drove away. When they came back later he was gone. He remained missing for five days until he was picked up next to a highway close by.

There is a bar called The Al'inn in the Nevada desert in the United States! It has a picture of an alien as its sign.

A Florida insurance company offers insurance against alien abduction.

Over 100 crop circles have been reported in Britain each year since 1988. They were between two and twenty metres across.

★ Almost all the people who say they have been abducted by aliens have had strong electric shocks earlier in their lives, such as being struck by lightning.

★ In 1996, Jesse Long, an American who claimed he had been abducted by aliens as a boy, had an operation to remove an "implant" at a hospital in Los Angeles. A clear triangular sliver was removed from the lower part of his right leg. When looked at by scientists, it was found to be glass.

★ In October 1996 a man from Dagenham, Essex, took out an insurance policy against being kidnapped by aliens.

The famous "Philadelphia Experiment" by the US Navy is said to have taken place in 1943. It happened at the harbour of the city of Philadelphia and later out to sea. A ship and the crew were made to disappear. A force field of some sort was put on the ship, a destroyer, and a green mist came up and covered the ship. The ship was said to have appeared and disappeared. At sea, the same thing happened. However, some of the men did not return at once and had to be brought back slowly. There were reports that some men became ill and some died. Later, some of the crew vanished at home, walking in the street or just sitting in public places, only to come back later. What happened to them was unexplained.

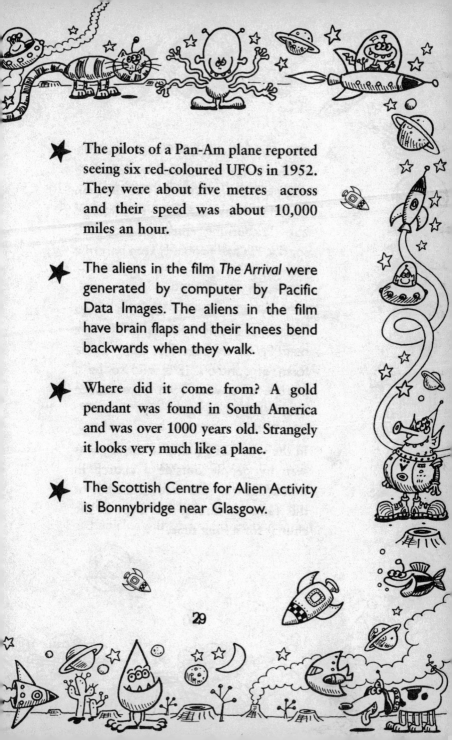

★ The pilots of a Pan-Am plane reported seeing six red-coloured UFOs in 1952. They were about five metres across and their speed was about 10,000 miles an hour.

★ The aliens in the film *The Arrival* were generated by computer by Pacific Data Images. The aliens in the film have brain flaps and their knees bend backwards when they walk.

★ Where did it come from? A gold pendant was found in South America and was over 1000 years old. Strangely it looks very much like a plane.

★ The Scottish Centre for Alien Activity is Bonnybridge near Glasgow.

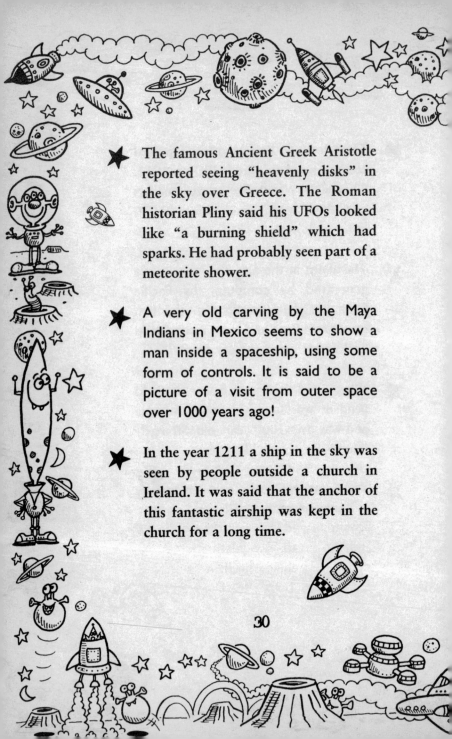

The famous Ancient Greek Aristotle reported seeing "heavenly disks" in the sky over Greece. The Roman historian Pliny said his UFOs looked like "a burning shield" which had sparks. He had probably seen part of a meteorite shower.

A very old carving by the Maya Indians in Mexico seems to show a man inside a spaceship, using some form of controls. It is said to be a picture of a visit from outer space over 1000 years ago!

In the year 1211 a ship in the sky was seen by people outside a church in Ireland. It was said that the anchor of this fantastic airship was kept in the church for a long time.

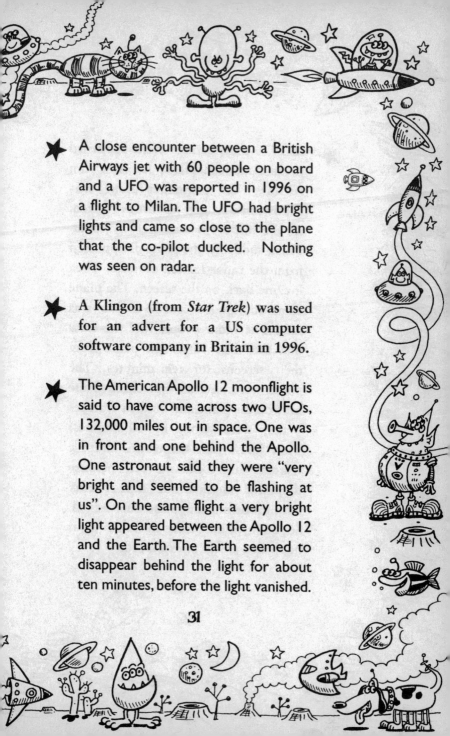

★ A close encounter between a British Airways jet with 60 people on board and a UFO was reported in 1996 on a flight to Milan. The UFO had bright lights and came so close to the plane that the co-pilot ducked. Nothing was seen on radar.

★ A Klingon (from *Star Trek*) was used for an advert for a US computer software company in Britain in 1996.

★ The American Apollo 12 moonflight is said to have come across two UFOs, 132,000 miles out in space. One was in front and one behind the Apollo. One astronaut said they were "very bright and seemed to be flashing at us". On the same flight a very bright light appeared between the Apollo 12 and the Earth. The Earth seemed to disappear behind the light for about ten minutes, before the light vanished.

31

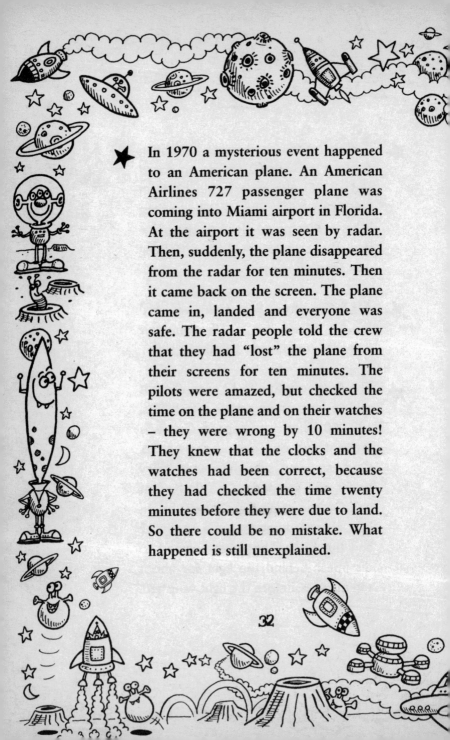

In 1970 a mysterious event happened to an American plane. An American Airlines 727 passenger plane was coming into Miami airport in Florida. At the airport it was seen by radar. Then, suddenly, the plane disappeared from the radar for ten minutes. Then it came back on the screen. The plane came in, landed and everyone was safe. The radar people told the crew that they had "lost" the plane from their screens for ten minutes. The pilots were amazed, but checked the time on the plane and on their watches – they were wrong by 10 minutes! They knew that the clocks and the watches had been correct, because they had checked the time twenty minutes before they were due to land. So there could be no mistake. What happened is still unexplained.

★ So many strange things were seen in the air over Europe in the Middle Ages that the two leading Emperors decided on laws against these "Tyrants of the Air". These unknown beings were said to kidnap people and take them away in the sky for a while. When the people came back, no one liked them, and they were all burned at the stake !

★ The American air force, the USAF, has often said that UFOs do not exist. What is odd, though, is that they tell pilots what to do if they see UFOs!

★ The Mars rock on which life was believed to have been found in 1996 was found in the Allan Hills in Antarctica in 1984. It was part of a meteorite from Mars.

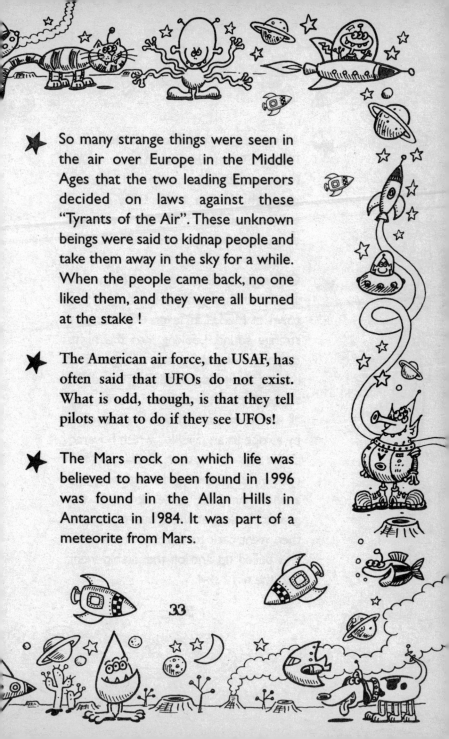

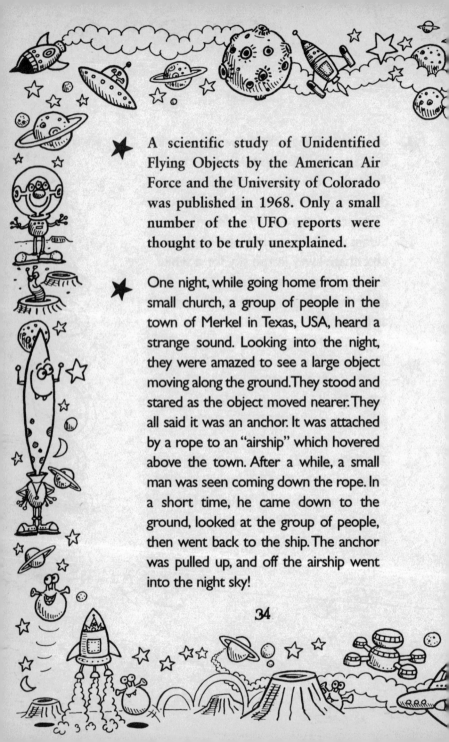

A scientific study of Unidentified Flying Objects by the American Air Force and the University of Colorado was published in 1968. Only a small number of the UFO reports were thought to be truly unexplained.

One night, while going home from their small church, a group of people in the town of Merkel in Texas, USA, heard a strange sound. Looking into the night, they were amazed to see a large object moving along the ground. They stood and stared as the object moved nearer. They all said it was an anchor. It was attached by a rope to an "airship" which hovered above the town. After a while, a small man was seen coming down the rope. In a short time, he came down to the ground, looked at the group of people, then went back to the ship. The anchor was pulled up, and off the airship went into the night sky!

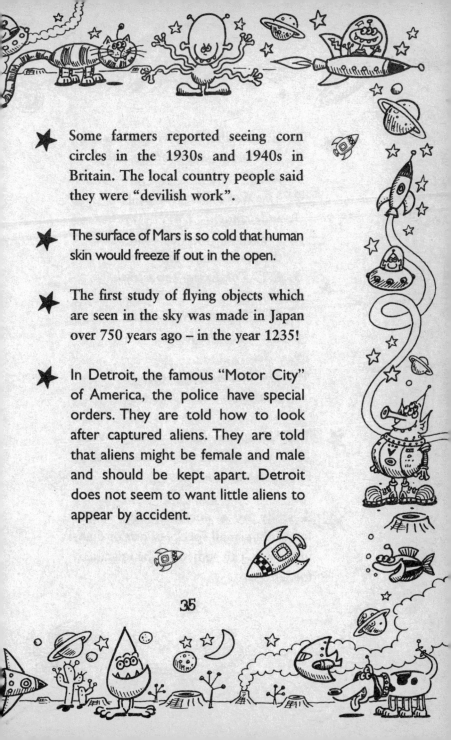

★ Some farmers reported seeing corn circles in the 1930s and 1940s in Britain. The local country people said they were "devilish work".

★ The surface of Mars is so cold that human skin would freeze if out in the open.

★ The first study of flying objects which are seen in the sky was made in Japan over 750 years ago – in the year 1235!

★ In Detroit, the famous "Motor City" of America, the police have special orders. They are told how to look after captured aliens. They are told that aliens might be female and male and should be kept apart. Detroit does not seem to want little aliens to appear by accident.

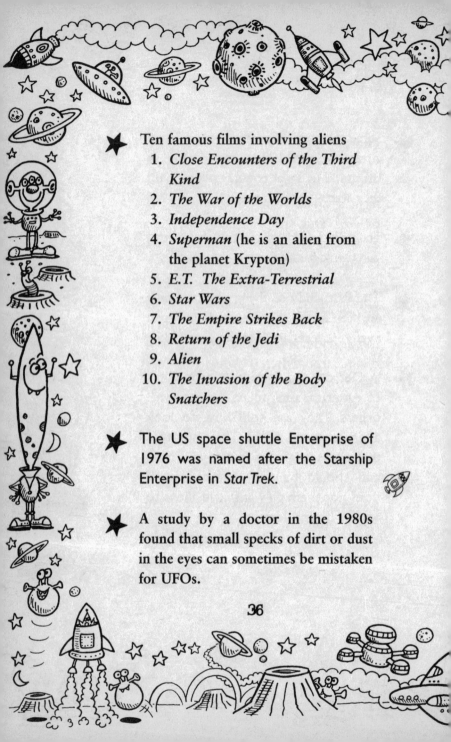

★ Ten famous films involving aliens
1. *Close Encounters of the Third Kind*
2. *The War of the Worlds*
3. *Independence Day*
4. *Superman* (he is an alien from the planet Krypton)
5. *E.T. The Extra-Terrestrial*
6. *Star Wars*
7. *The Empire Strikes Back*
8. *Return of the Jedi*
9. *Alien*
10. *The Invasion of the Body Snatchers*

★ The US space shuttle Enterprise of 1976 was named after the Starship Enterprise in *Star Trek*.

★ A study by a doctor in the 1980s found that small specks of dirt or dust in the eyes can sometimes be mistaken for UFOs.

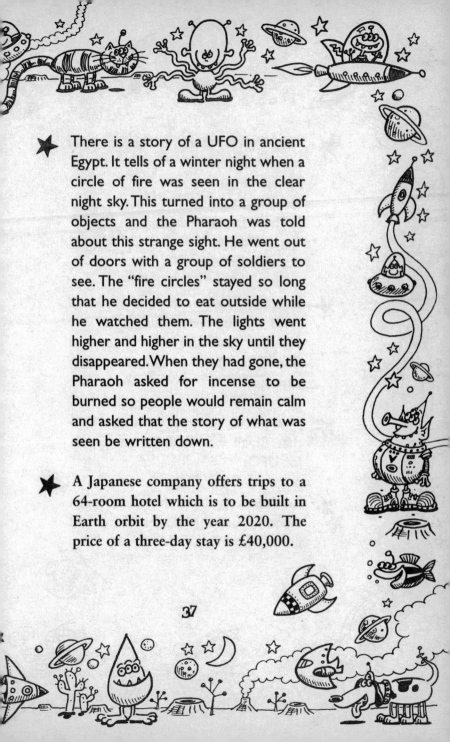

There is a story of a UFO in ancient Egypt. It tells of a winter night when a circle of fire was seen in the clear night sky. This turned into a group of objects and the Pharaoh was told about this strange sight. He went out of doors with a group of soldiers to see. The "fire circles" stayed so long that he decided to eat outside while he watched them. The lights went higher and higher in the sky until they disappeared. When they had gone, the Pharaoh asked for incense to be burned so people would remain calm and asked that the story of what was seen be written down.

A Japanese company offers trips to a 64-room hotel which is to be built in Earth orbit by the year 2020. The price of a three-day stay is £40,000.

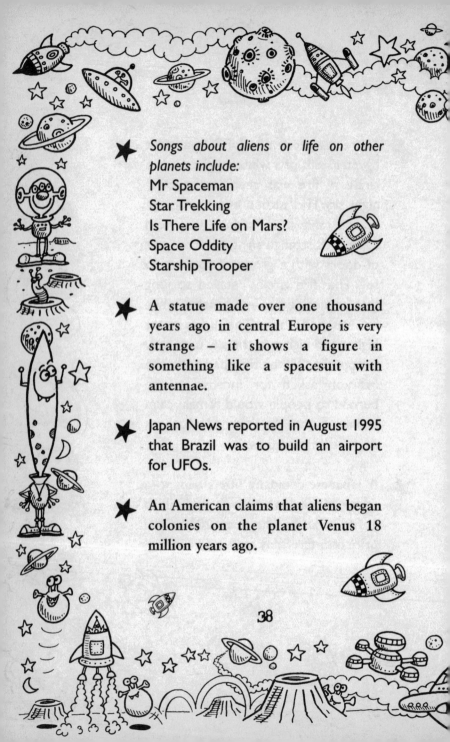

★ *Songs about aliens or life on other planets include:*
Mr Spaceman
Star Trekking
Is There Life on Mars?
Space Oddity
Starship Trooper

★ A statue made over one thousand years ago in central Europe is very strange – it shows a figure in something like a spacesuit with antennae.

★ Japan News reported in August 1995 that Brazil was to build an airport for UFOs.

★ An American claims that aliens began colonies on the planet Venus 18 million years ago.

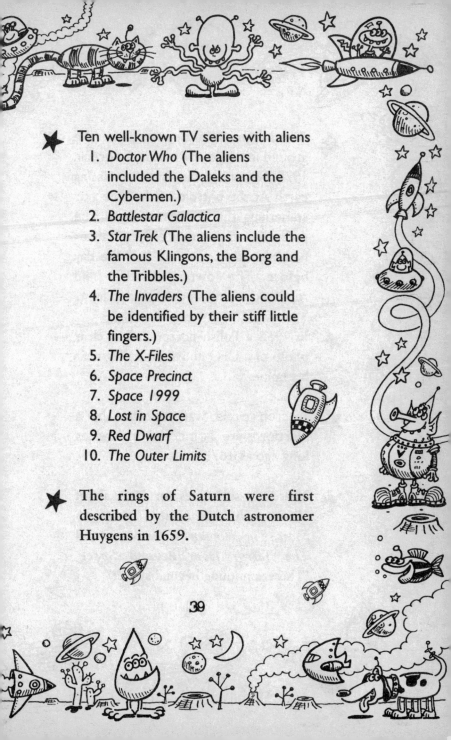

⭐ Ten well-known TV series with aliens
  1. *Doctor Who* (The aliens included the Daleks and the Cybermen.)
  2. *Battlestar Galactica*
  3. *Star Trek* (The aliens include the famous Klingons, the Borg and the Tribbles.)
  4. *The Invaders* (The aliens could be identified by their stiff little fingers.)
  5. *The X-Files*
  6. *Space Precinct*
  7. *Space 1999*
  8. *Lost in Space*
  9. *Red Dwarf*
  10. *The Outer Limits*

⭐ The rings of Saturn were first described by the Dutch astronomer Huygens in 1659.

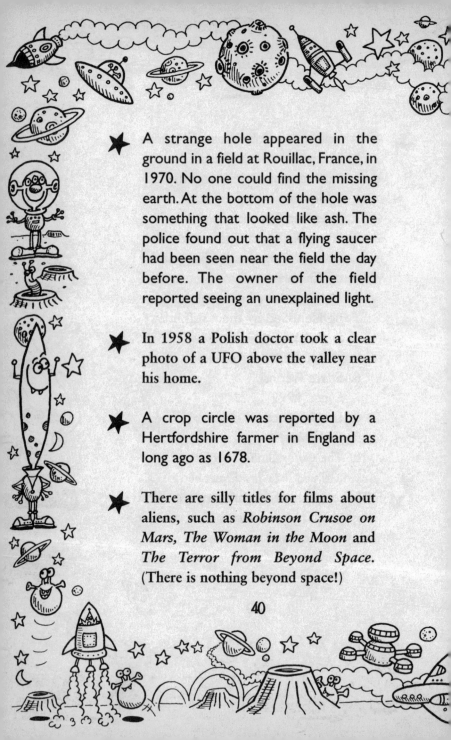

A strange hole appeared in the ground in a field at Rouillac, France, in 1970. No one could find the missing earth. At the bottom of the hole was something that looked like ash. The police found out that a flying saucer had been seen near the field the day before. The owner of the field reported seeing an unexplained light.

In 1958 a Polish doctor took a clear photo of a UFO above the valley near his home.

A crop circle was reported by a Hertfordshire farmer in England as long ago as 1678.

There are silly titles for films about aliens, such as *Robinson Crusoe on Mars*, *The Woman in the Moon* and *The Terror from Beyond Space*. (There is nothing beyond space!)

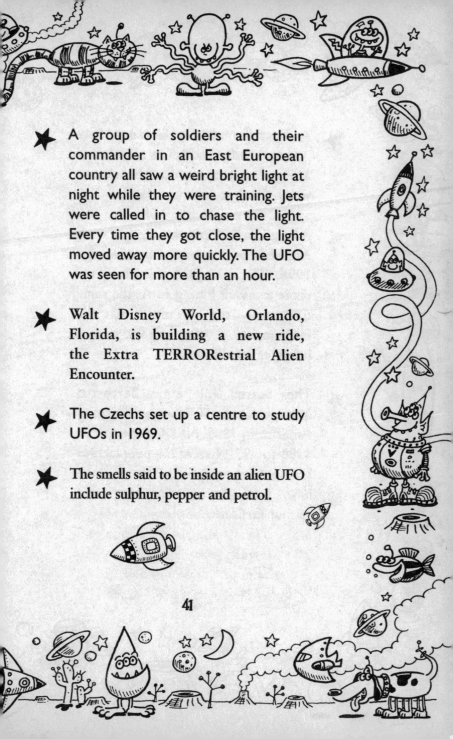

★ A group of soldiers and their commander in an East European country all saw a weird bright light at night while they were training. Jets were called in to chase the light. Every time they got close, the light moved away more quickly. The UFO was seen for more than an hour.

★ Walt Disney World, Orlando, Florida, is building a new ride, the Extra TERRORestrial Alien Encounter.

★ The Czechs set up a centre to study UFOs in 1969.

★ The smells said to be inside an alien UFO include sulphur, pepper and petrol.

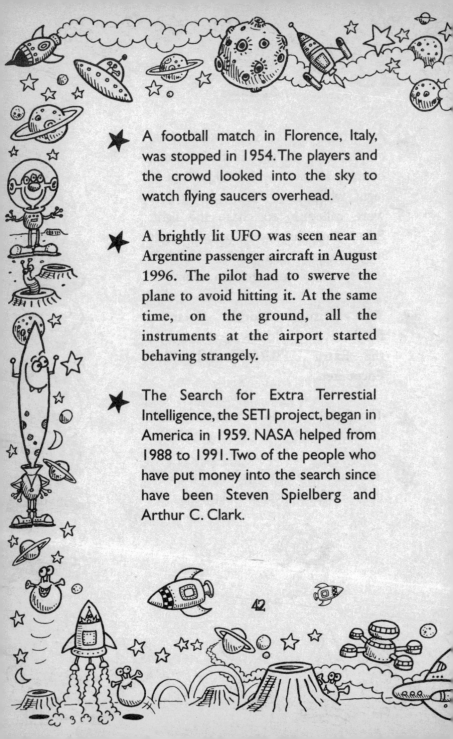

A football match in Florence, Italy, was stopped in 1954. The players and the crowd looked into the sky to watch flying saucers overhead.

A brightly lit UFO was seen near an Argentine passenger aircraft in August 1996. The pilot had to swerve the plane to avoid hitting it. At the same time, on the ground, all the instruments at the airport started behaving strangely.

The Search for Extra Terrestial Intelligence, the SETI project, began in America in 1959. NASA helped from 1988 to 1991. Two of the people who have put money into the search since have been Steven Spielberg and Arthur C. Clark.

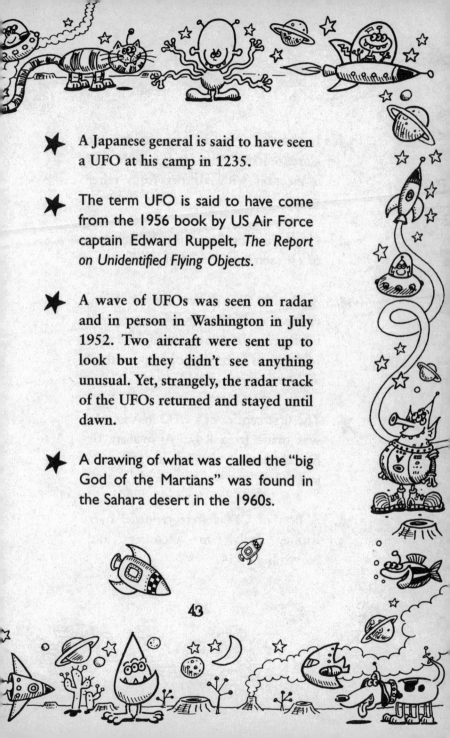

★ A Japanese general is said to have seen a UFO at his camp in 1235.

★ The term UFO is said to have come from the 1956 book by US Air Force captain Edward Ruppelt, *The Report on Unidentified Flying Objects*.

★ A wave of UFOs was seen on radar and in person in Washington in July 1952. Two aircraft were sent up to look but they didn't see anything unusual. Yet, strangely, the radar track of the UFOs returned and stayed until dawn.

★ A drawing of what was called the "big God of the Martians" was found in the Sahara desert in the 1960s.

In 1491, a maths expert, Jerome Cardan, from Milan, Italy, said he had a meeting with visitors from outer space.

Magic Fire, or flames in the sea, are often seen with UFOs in Japan.

A British taxi driver, George King, claimed contact with extraterrestrial intelligence in 1954. He said he was told he was to be the voice on Earth of an interplanetary "parliament".

The first report of a UFO in Australia was made by a Royal Australian Air Force pilot off the Tasman peninsula in 1942.

A fleet of UFOs were reported over Rome, Italy, in October and November 1954.

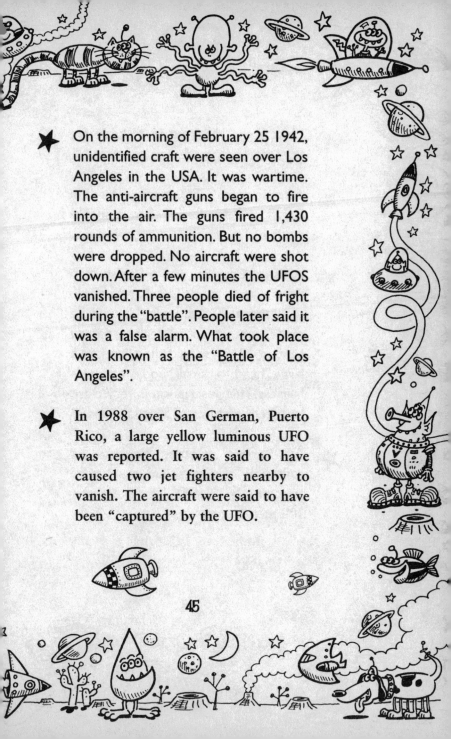

★ On the morning of February 25 1942, unidentified craft were seen over Los Angeles in the USA. It was wartime. The anti-aircraft guns began to fire into the air. The guns fired 1,430 rounds of ammunition. But no bombs were dropped. No aircraft were shot down. After a few minutes the UFOS vanished. Three people died of fright during the "battle". People later said it was a false alarm. What took place was known as the "Battle of Los Angeles".

★ In 1988 over San German, Puerto Rico, a large yellow luminous UFO was reported. It was said to have caused two jet fighters nearby to vanish. The aircraft were said to have been "captured" by the UFO.

45

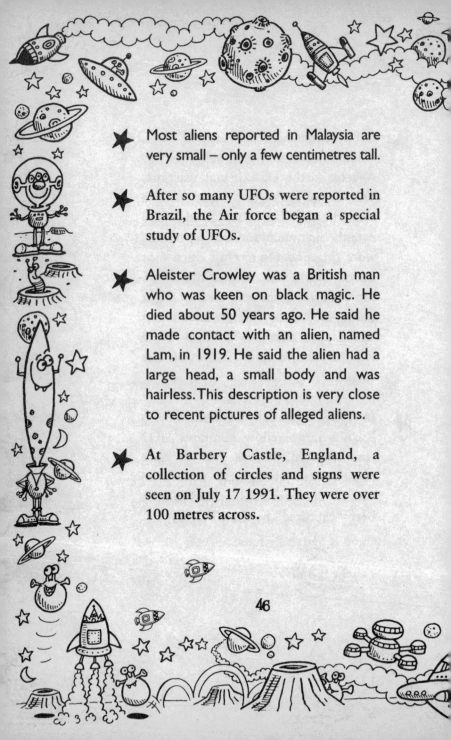

★ Most aliens reported in Malaysia are very small – only a few centimetres tall.

★ After so many UFOs were reported in Brazil, the Air force began a special study of UFOs.

★ Aleister Crowley was a British man who was keen on black magic. He died about 50 years ago. He said he made contact with an alien, named Lam, in 1919. He said the alien had a large head, a small body and was hairless. This description is very close to recent pictures of alleged aliens.

★ At Barbery Castle, England, a collection of circles and signs were seen on July 17 1991. They were over 100 metres across.

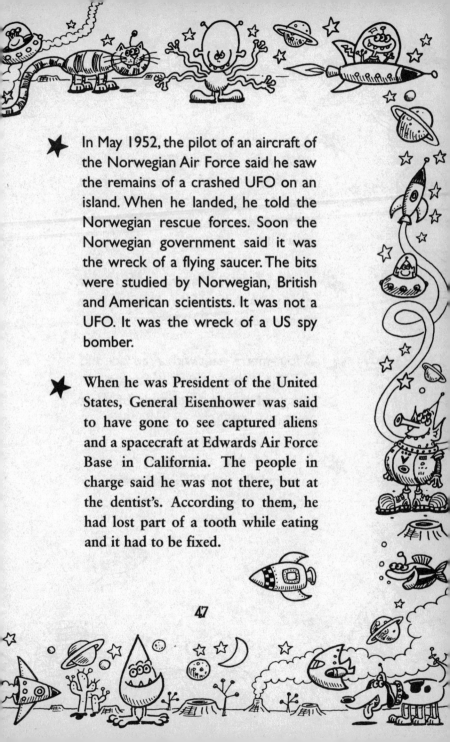

★ In May 1952, the pilot of an aircraft of the Norwegian Air Force said he saw the remains of a crashed UFO on an island. When he landed, he told the Norwegian rescue forces. Soon the Norwegian government said it was the wreck of a flying saucer. The bits were studied by Norwegian, British and American scientists. It was not a UFO. It was the wreck of a US spy bomber.

★ When he was President of the United States, General Eisenhower was said to have gone to see captured aliens and a spacecraft at Edwards Air Force Base in California. The people in charge said he was not there, but at the dentist's. According to them, he had lost part of a tooth while eating and it had to be fixed.

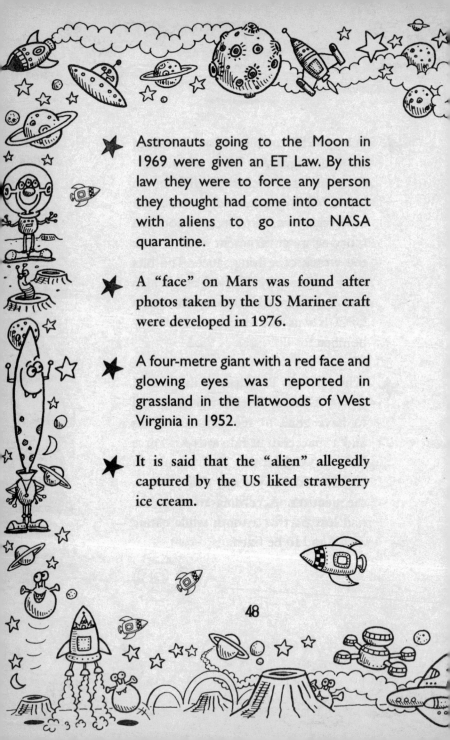

★ Astronauts going to the Moon in 1969 were given an ET Law. By this law they were to force any person they thought had come into contact with aliens to go into NASA quarantine.

★ A "face" on Mars was found after photos taken by the US Mariner craft were developed in 1976.

★ A four-metre giant with a red face and glowing eyes was reported in grassland in the Flatwoods of West Virginia in 1952.

★ It is said that the "alien" allegedly captured by the US liked strawberry ice cream.

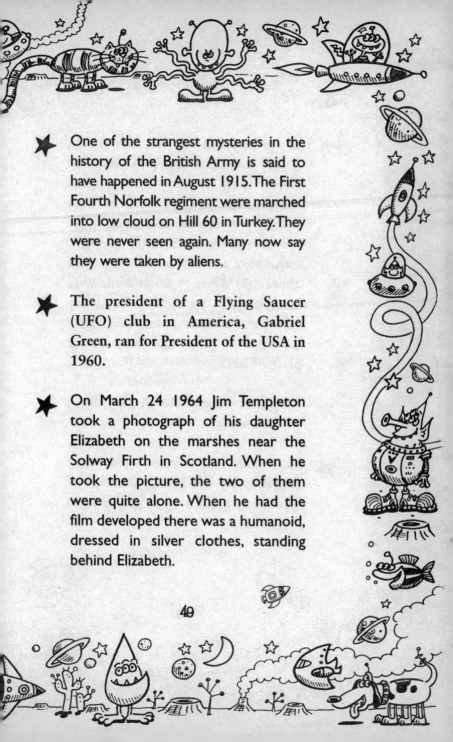

★ One of the strangest mysteries in the history of the British Army is said to have happened in August 1915. The First Fourth Norfolk regiment were marched into low cloud on Hill 60 in Turkey. They were never seen again. Many now say they were taken by aliens.

★ The president of a Flying Saucer (UFO) club in America, Gabriel Green, ran for President of the USA in 1960.

★ On March 24 1964 Jim Templeton took a photograph of his daughter Elizabeth on the marshes near the Solway Firth in Scotland. When he took the picture, the two of them were quite alone. When he had the film developed there was a humanoid, dressed in silver clothes, standing behind Elizabeth.

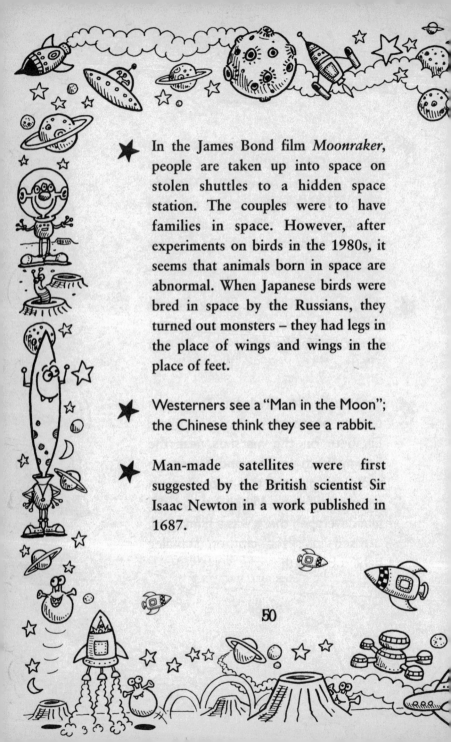

In the James Bond film *Moonraker*, people are taken up into space on stolen shuttles to a hidden space station. The couples were to have families in space. However, after experiments on birds in the 1980s, it seems that animals born in space are abnormal. When Japanese birds were bred in space by the Russians, they turned out monsters – they had legs in the place of wings and wings in the place of feet.

Westerners see a "Man in the Moon"; the Chinese think they see a rabbit.

Man-made satellites were first suggested by the British scientist Sir Isaac Newton in a work published in 1687.

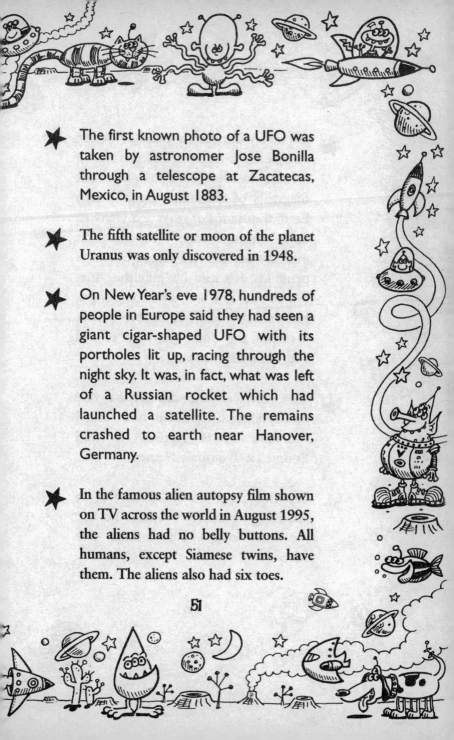

The first known photo of a UFO was taken by astronomer Jose Bonilla through a telescope at Zacatecas, Mexico, in August 1883.

The fifth satellite or moon of the planet Uranus was only discovered in 1948.

On New Year's eve 1978, hundreds of people in Europe said they had seen a giant cigar-shaped UFO with its portholes lit up, racing through the night sky. It was, in fact, what was left of a Russian rocket which had launched a satellite. The remains crashed to earth near Hanover, Germany.

In the famous alien autopsy film shown on TV across the world in August 1995, the aliens had no belly buttons. All humans, except Siamese twins, have them. The aliens also had six toes.

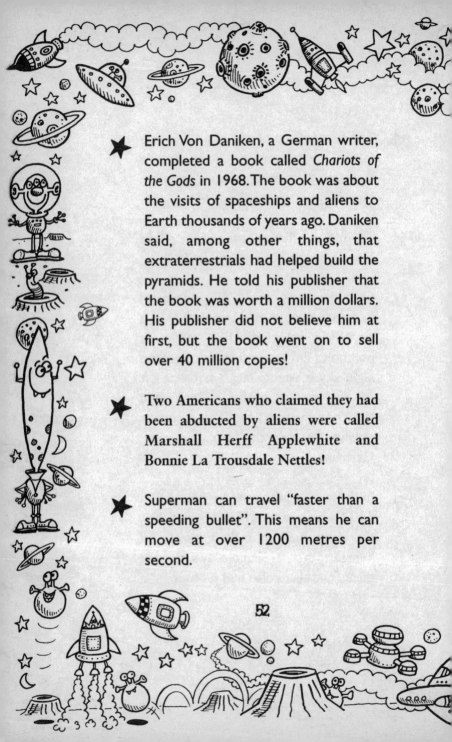

Erich Von Daniken, a German writer, completed a book called *Chariots of the Gods* in 1968. The book was about the visits of spaceships and aliens to Earth thousands of years ago. Daniken said, among other things, that extraterrestrials had helped build the pyramids. He told his publisher that the book was worth a million dollars. His publisher did not believe him at first, but the book went on to sell over 40 million copies!

Two Americans who claimed they had been abducted by aliens were called Marshall Herff Applewhite and Bonnie La Trousdale Nettles!

Superman can travel "faster than a speeding bullet". This means he can move at over 1200 metres per second.

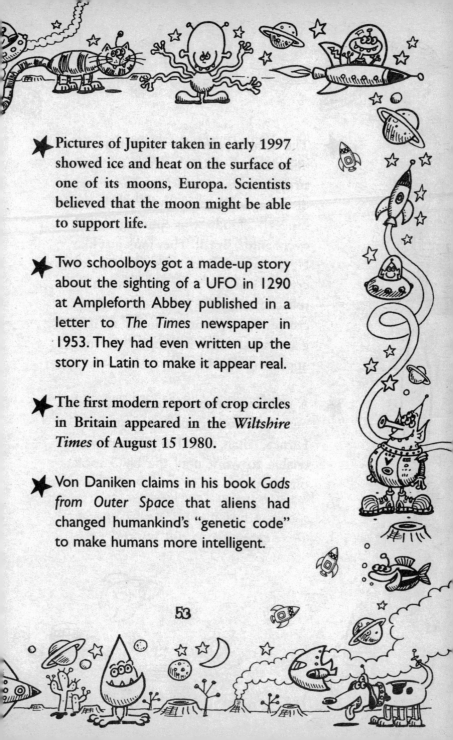

★ Pictures of Jupiter taken in early 1997 showed ice and heat on the surface of one of its moons, Europa. Scientists believed that the moon might be able to support life.

★ Two schoolboys got a made-up story about the sighting of a UFO in 1290 at Ampleforth Abbey published in a letter to *The Times* newspaper in 1953. They had even written up the story in Latin to make it appear real.

★ The first modern report of crop circles in Britain appeared in the *Wiltshire Times* of August 15 1980.

★ Von Daniken claims in his book *Gods from Outer Space* that aliens had changed humankind's "genetic code" to make humans more intelligent.

The weather can play tricks that are mistaken for UFOs, visions and strange lights. Clouds can form into disc shapes. A group of these "flying saucer" clouds was photographed over Santos, Brazil. They look just like UFOs from a distance. In cold air ice crystals can pile into columns which reflect sunlight. When a snow cloud crosses the column, it looks as if a giant cross, which is lit up by the sun, appears in the sky.

A UFO was reported to have landed near an electric power station in Eureka, Utah, US. The station was unable to work until the UFO took off again.

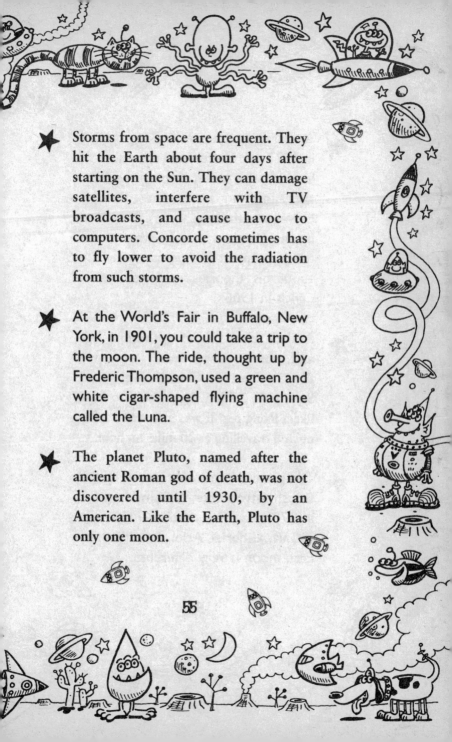

★ Storms from space are frequent. They hit the Earth about four days after starting on the Sun. They can damage satellites, interfere with TV broadcasts, and cause havoc to computers. Concorde sometimes has to fly lower to avoid the radiation from such storms.

★ At the World's Fair in Buffalo, New York, in 1901, you could take a trip to the moon. The ride, thought up by Frederic Thompson, used a green and white cigar-shaped flying machine called the Luna.

★ The planet Pluto, named after the ancient Roman god of death, was not discovered until 1930, by an American. Like the Earth, Pluto has only one moon.

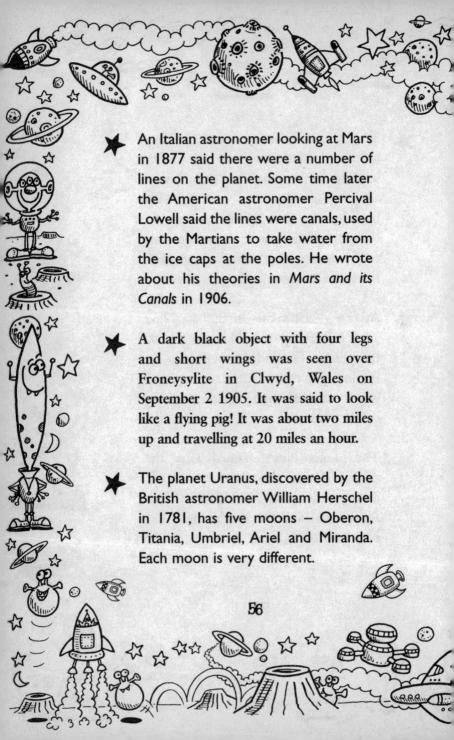

An Italian astronomer looking at Mars in 1877 said there were a number of lines on the planet. Some time later the American astronomer Percival Lowell said the lines were canals, used by the Martians to take water from the ice caps at the poles. He wrote about his theories in *Mars and its Canals* in 1906.

A dark black object with four legs and short wings was seen over Froneysylite in Clwyd, Wales on September 2 1905. It was said to look like a flying pig! It was about two miles up and travelling at 20 miles an hour.

The planet Uranus, discovered by the British astronomer William Herschel in 1781, has five moons – Oberon, Titania, Umbriel, Ariel and Miranda. Each moon is very different.

★ Ten famous stories about Martians and other aliens

1. *The War of the Worlds* by H. G. Wells
2. *The Martian Chronicles* by Ray Bradbury
3. *A Princess of Mars* by Edgar Rice Burroughs (famous for Tarzan)
4. *The Hitchhiker's Guide to the Galaxy* by Douglas Adams
5. *Planet of the Apes* by Pierre Boulle
6. *Out of the Silent Planet* by C. S. Lewis
7. *Foundation* by Isaac Asimov
8. *Childhood's End* by Arthur C. Clarke
9. *Dune* by Frank Herbert
10. *The Day of the Triffids* by John Wyndham

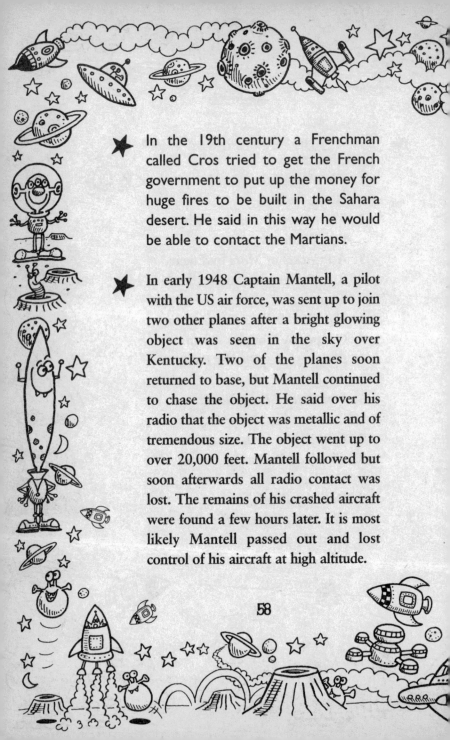

★ In the 19th century a Frenchman called Cros tried to get the French government to put up the money for huge fires to be built in the Sahara desert. He said in this way he would be able to contact the Martians.

★ In early 1948 Captain Mantell, a pilot with the US air force, was sent up to join two other planes after a bright glowing object was seen in the sky over Kentucky. Two of the planes soon returned to base, but Mantell continued to chase the object. He said over his radio that the object was metallic and of tremendous size. The object went up to over 20,000 feet. Mantell followed but soon afterwards all radio contact was lost. The remains of his crashed aircraft were found a few hours later. It is most likely Mantell passed out and lost control of his aircraft at high altitude.

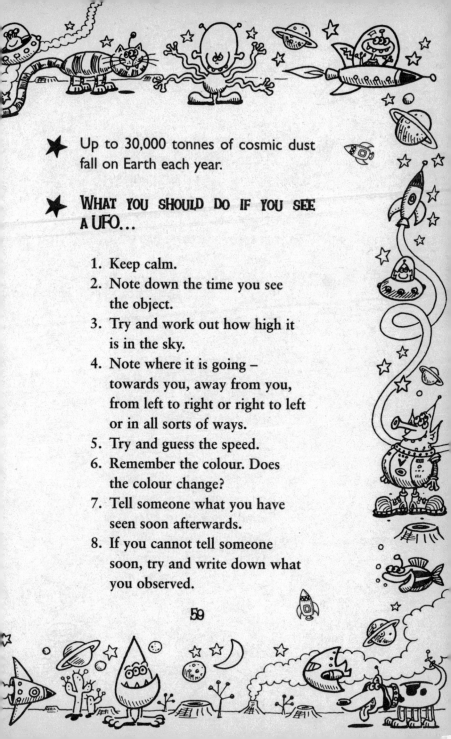

★ Up to 30,000 tonnes of cosmic dust fall on Earth each year.

★ ### WHAT YOU SHOULD DO IF YOU SEE A UFO...

1. Keep calm.
2. Note down the time you see the object.
3. Try and work out how high it is in the sky.
4. Note where it is going – towards you, away from you, from left to right or right to left or in all sorts of ways.
5. Try and guess the speed.
6. Remember the colour. Does the colour change?
7. Tell someone what you have seen soon afterwards.
8. If you cannot tell someone soon, try and write down what you observed.

Also published by Macmillan

FACT ATTACK

BEASTLY BODIES

DID YOU KNOW THAT . . .

The human body loses enough heat in an hour to boil half a gallon of water.

If calcium is taken out of human bones, they become so rubbery that they can be tied in a knot like rope or string.

The city with the highest number of babies born in taxis is New York, USA.

A giraffe has the same number of bones in its neck as a human does.

Richard III of England, Louis XIV of France and the Emperor Napoleon of France were all born with teeth.

Also published by Macmillan

FACT ATTACK

FANTASTIC FOOTBALL

DID YOU KNOW THAT . . .

James I of England was probably the first king to
attend a game of football.

In the 1966 World Cup final, Geoff Hurst scored
three goals — one with a header, one with his left
foot and one with his right foot!

Millwall's fanzine is called *No One Likes Us*.

When Uruguay won the World Cup in 1930 the
whole country was given a day off.

After a survey three years ago, it was found
Scottish footballers have one leg shorter than
the other!

Fact Attack titles available from Macmillan

The prices shown below are correct at the time of going to press. However, Macmillan Publishers reserve the right to show new retail prices on covers which may differ from those previously advertised.

Awesome Aliens	**Ian Locke**	**£1.99**
Beastly Bodies	**Ian Locke**	**£1.99**
Crazy Creatures	**Ian Locke**	**£1.99**
Fantastic Football	**Ian Locke**	**£1.99**
Dastardly Deeds	**Ian Locke**	**£1.99**
Cool Cars	**Ian Locke**	**£1.99**
Gruesome Ghosts	**Ian Locke**	**£1.99**
Dreadful Disasters	**Ian Locke**	**£1.99**
Mad Medicine	**Ian Locke**	**£1.99**
Nutty Numbers	**Rowland Morgan**	**£1.99**

All Macmillan titles can be ordered at your local bookshop or are available by post from:

**Book Service by Post
PO Box 29, Douglas, Isle of Man IM99 1BQ**

Credit cards accepted. For details:
Telephone: 01624 675137
Fax: 01624 670923
E-mail: bookshop@enterprise.net

Free postage and packing in the UK.
Overseas customers: add £1 per book (paperback)
and £3 per book (hardback).

Sue Gerhardt is a practising psychoanalytic psychotherapist. She wrote the bestselling *Why Love Matters*, an accessible account of the neuroscience of early development.

Further praise for *The Selfish Society*

'A brilliant critique of why we stopped loving each other and made money instead'
Oliver James, *Psychologies Magazine*

'The idea that broken Britain might be mended with cuddles will attract cynicism, but Gerhardt has the neuroscience to back it up . . . offering insights into the critical importance of the values learnt in early life'
Financial Times

'If we don't change the way we bring up children, beginning from the moment that they are born, we will stay depressed and in debt, Gerhardt says. I think I believe her'
Independent on Sunday

Also by Sue Gerhardt

Why Love Matters: how affection
shapes a baby's brain